# Teaching With Favorite
# I SPY Books

BY JOAN NOVELLI

SCHOLASTIC
PROFESSIONAL BOOKS

NEW YORK • TORONTO • LONDON • AUCKLAND • SYDNEY
MEXICO CITY • NEW DELHI • HONG KONG • BUENOS AIRES

## Acknowledgments

From I SPY: A BOOK OF PICTURE RIDDLES by Jean Marzollo, photographs by Walter Wick.
Text copyright © 1992 by Jean Marzollo. Photographs copyright © 1992 by Walter Wick.

From I SPY FUN HOUSE by Jean Marzollo, photographs by Walter Wick.
Text copyright © 1993 by Jean Marzollo. Photographs copyright © 1993 by Walter Wick.

From I SPY MYSTERY by Jean Marzollo, photographs by Walter Wick.
Text copyright © 1993 by Jean Marzollo. Photographs copyright © 1993 by Walter Wick.

From I SPY FANTASY by Jean Marzollo, photographs by Walter Wick.
Text copyright © 1994 by Jean Marzollo. Photographs copyright © 1994 by Walter Wick.

From I SPY SCHOOL DAYS by Jean Marzollo, photographs by Walter Wick.
Text copyright © 1995 by Jean Marzollo. Photographs copyright © 1995 by Walter Wick.

From I SPY SPOOKY NIGHT by Jean Marzollo, photographs by Walter Wick.
Text copyright © 1995 by Jean Marzollo. Photographs copyright © 1995 by Walter Wick.

From I SPY TREASURE HUNT by Jean Marzollo, photographs by Walter Wick.
Text copyright © 1999 by Jean Marzollo. Photographs copyright © 1999 by Walter Wick.

From I SPY SUPER CHALLENGER! by Jean Marzollo, photographs by Walter Wick.
Text copyright © 1997 by Jean Marzollo. Cover illustration copyright © 1997 by Walter Wick.

From I SPY GOLD CHALLENGER! by Jean Marzollo, photographs by Walter Wick.
Text copyright © 1998 by Jean Marzollo. Cover illustration copyright © 1998 by Walter Wick.

From I SPY EXTREME CHALLENGER! by Jean Marzollo, photographs by Walter Wick.
Text copyright © 2000 by Jean Marzollo. Cover illustration copyright © 2000 by Walter Wick.

Cover and interior design by **Holly Grundon**
Interior illustrations by **Cary Pillo**

ISBN: 0-439-33166-8

1 2 3 4 5 6 7 8 9 10    40    09 08 07 06 05 04 03

# Contents

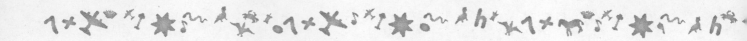

# About This Book

**I** visited the library with my son a while back to look for an I Spy book. The children's librarian was surprised that we found it on the shelves. "They're the most borrowed books," she said. It showed in the worn pages of the copy of *I Spy School Days* that my son was holding.

I Spy books have been a favorite with children since they first came out. What makes them so popular? From a young age, children are captivated by activities that let them figure things out. Like the puzzles and treasure hunts children love, the intriguing riddles on each I Spy page offer endless opportunities to figure things out. Along the way, children can build a range of skills, including:

**Observing:** As children scour each picture trying to find all the items in the riddles, they'll discover interesting details—for example, in *I Spy Treasure Hunt*, children will discover that one of three ducks can be found in the form of a duck-shaped pond.

**Making Comparisons:** It's interesting to explore the way objects in the pictures relate in size. For example, in *I Spy Spooky Night*, a fence is constructed from clothespins, giving children a sense of how big the tree and other objects in the picture are.

**Sorting and Classifying:** How are objects on a page alike and different? Children can find endless ways to sort objects in a picture. In *I Spy School Days*, various objects are sorted into Venn diagram–like circles; the last part of the riddle challenges children to find places for all the objects remaining outside the circles.

**Problem-Solving and Creative Thinking:** Children are fascinated by the intricate pictures in each I Spy book—it's fun to take apart the pictures in their minds and try to imagine how each set was constructed. For example, in *I Spy Fantasy*, they might wonder what the clouds are made of or how they "float" in the sky. Children may enjoy testing some of their ideas.

**E**ach I Spy book is filled with invitations like this to think, explore, discover, and learn. Whatever level of challenge children take on, the rewards are rich. As they successfully solve the riddles, children develop a sense of satisfaction and confidence in their abilities, which will help them tackle new, sometimes tougher challenges that come their way at home and in school.

—*Joan Novelli*

# Teaching With the Activities in This Book

From activities that reinforce spelling skills to those that strengthen math and science skills and concepts, you'll be amazed at the many ways you can use I Spy books to support your curriculum—all the while giving your students more of what they love about these favorite books. This book features ten I Spy titles and activities to connect with your curriculum and inspire your students to challenge themselves in their learning.

You can use the activities in this book in many ways—for example, as a special activity when you have a few extra minutes or as the focus of a learning center that changes each week or two. More on these and other ideas follows.

**Share I Spy Morning Messages:** For a change of pace, use an I Spy book as the focus of your morning message or daily letter. Open an I Spy book to a picture and display it on an easel next to your morning message pad. In your message to children, invite them to find something in the picture. For example, a picture might lend itself to naming something for each letter of the alphabet. (See page 51.) Other morning message ideas include:

◎ Estimate the number of objects in the picture.

◎ Choose a word from the riddle. Write a word that rhymes with it.

◎ Find something in the picture that starts with the same first letter of your name. Write them both.

**Take an I Spy Break:** Many of the activities in this book are just right for those times that students need a break between more involved lessons, or when you just have a few free minutes. Students will also enjoy having I Spy time built into their daily routine. You might make an I Spy activity a regular part of your morning circle time, or you might build it into another part of your schedule—for example, setting aside five minutes after math, before lunch, or at the end of the day to enjoy an I Spy activity.

**Set Up an I Spy Center:** Children will delight in a classroom I Spy center. Introduce a different book in the center every week or so, along with activities from the book that you've copied on chart paper or activity cards. Some of the activities use reproducible pages—for example, Classroom Cubbies lets children create an original I Spy picture and riddle based on one in *I Spy: A Book of Picture Riddles*. (See page 14.) Plan ahead for these so that you have copies of the reproducible pages ready.

**Create an I Spy Interactive Display:** Use a large white board as a temporary display area. Display an I Spy book on the tray, along with some markers. Invite children to notice objects in the book that are not mentioned in the riddles. Have them write new I Spy riddles on the board for their classmates to solve—for example, "I spy something that rhymes with *ring*."

**I Spy Incubator:** Think about setting up a corner of your classroom as an I Spy incubator. Talk about the ways Walter Wick built the scenes that became each I Spy picture. Gather everyday and unusual objects from around the classroom. Invite children, with permission, to bring in more from home. Place items in the I Spy area and let children take over, using their imagination and creative thinking skills to come up with a collaborative I Spy set. (This might connect with an area of study—for example, "I Spy Under the Sea.") Have children write riddles to go with the sets. Be sure to photograph each set before dismantling it to make space for a new one.

# I SPY Challenger Series

The I Spy Challenger books (*I Spy Super Challenger!*, *I Spy Gold Challenger!*, and *I Spy Extreme Challenger!*) feature favorite pictures from other I Spy books, with new riddles that require children to take a closer and more creative look at the objects on each page. It's interesting to notice what children observe the first time around with these pictures, and then again when they solve the new riddles. Children will be amazed at how much eludes them at first, and how much more they see with another look. Use these books to inspire children to make more "challenger" riddles. Let children choose favorite pictures from I Spy books and write new riddles that will give their classmates a visual and mental workout. (Of course, this means that they need to give their own skills a workout first to find new and elusive objects.)

**Jean Marzollo**

**Walter Wick**

Jean Marzollo and Walter Wick have been collaborating since 1991, when they decided to put their creative talents together to create *I Spy: A Book of Picture Riddles*. Jean, who was then editor of the kindergarten magazine *Let's Find Out* (Scholastic), had seen one of Walter's photographs—an image of screws, paperclips, and other "odds and ends" that he arranged carefully (for hours!) and then captured in a photograph. Inspired by this photo, Jean asked Walter to photograph colorful fasteners, such as buttons and paperclips, for a *Let's Find Out* poster. Some years later, they began work together on *I Spy: A Book of Picture Riddles*. How many different kinds of fasteners can your students find in the picture called "Odds & Ends"?

"I enjoy all the steps of the creative process. I like getting ideas, writing, and revising; I even like punctuation! To see the caterpillar of an idea slowly change into the butterfly of a book is a thrill to me every time."

—Jean Marzollo

Each I Spy riddle is like a tiny poem. Jean was drawn to poetry from an early age. "I loved to hear my grandmother, mother, and father recite poems from memory, and I loved to read. One of my favorite books was *A Child's Garden of Verses* by Robert Louis Stevenson." Each of the rhyming riddles in the I Spy books is written in a 3/4 waltz rhythm. Jean tests her riddles by singing them aloud to an old-fashioned song called "Sweet Betsy From Pike." "If you get your music teacher to teach you this song," she tells children, "you can test your I Spy riddles this way, too!"

Like Jean, Walter's creative inspiration comes from childhood interests. "We loved exploring the nearby woods. Sometimes I would find objects I could use for home-made projects. I loved to tinker and build." Walter's interest in art grew and he went on to study photography in college. As a lab technician and assistant to a commercial photographer, Walter became fascinated with the challenges of capturing shiny surfaces, shadows, and highlights in photographs. This passion for visual perception is seen in each spellbinding I Spy scene. The I Spy riddles invite children to discover some of the visual tricks embedded in each picture, such as a clothespin man, an ice-cream scoop bridge, and a bottle-cap lantern top. Children love to keep going, uncovering more of the secrets woven into each puzzling picture.

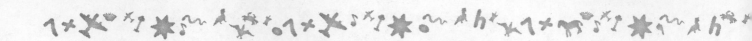

## Teaching Activities for Any Time

Use the activities that follow to enrich your students' experiences with any of the I Spy books.

### I Spy Up Close

Loop a string around the inside cover of your I Spy books and attach a magnifying glass. The magnifier will remind children to take a close look at the pictures and invite them to observe what they see in greater detail.

### Write I Spy Riddles

One of the most natural extension activities to use with I Spy books is, of course, to write new riddles for the pictures. Share these tips to help students get their riddles just right!

## Tip

To assist students in creating rhyming riddles like the ones in I Spy books, share the *Scholastic Rhyming Dictionary*, by Sue Young (Scholastic, 1997). This child-friendly reference book is organized by vowel sounds and final syllables and features more than 15,000 words.

- When you're looking for a rhyming word, try going through the letters of the alphabet from A to Z. A rhyming dictionary can help, too! (See Tip, left.)
- Jean Marzollo's riddles follow a pattern. Each I Spy line has four measures and each measure has three beats, or accented syllables. Clap out the pattern in an I Spy riddle. Encourage children to listen for the rhythm in riddles they write.
- Look for examples of alliteration (the same beginning sound, as in "a checker, a chair, and a chalkboard chart") and assonance (the same internal sound, as in "an ice skate, a rake, two bracelets…") in I Spy books. Let children try these devices with their own riddles.

### Countdown

Play Countdown. Set a timer for one minute. Begin by describing an item in the picture without naming it. Continue using words to describe the item until someone guesses it. Then move on to a new object. How many can you do in a minute? Let children take over, describing objects for classmates to guess.

### Spyglass Finders

Students will have fun using paper towel tube spyglasses to find even the most elusive objects in an I Spy picture. Have children make spyglasses by covering paper towel tubes with construction paper or foil and decorating them. Let them look through the spyglasses to see each picture from a different perspective.

## Sticky Note Challengers

Use sticky notes to invite children to discover something extra-challenging in
I Spy pictures. Put a sticky note on an I Spy picture. At the top, write "I Spy
Challenge." On the note, write a clue that indicates something you want
children to discover in the picture. To encourage attention to detail, observation skills, and creative thinking, go for an object that is hidden in some way or
disguised as something else—for example, on page 9 of *I Spy Treasure Hunt*, ask
children to find a penny. Using the penny as a clue, can they tell how tall the
trash can in the picture is? (*less than an inch*) To make a connection to a word
family you're teaching, ask students to find objects that represent rhyming
words. For example, on pages 18 and 19 of *I Spy Mystery*, ask children to find
sets of objects that represent rhyming words for the phonograms *-at* (*cat, hat*),
*-ouse* (*house, mouse*), and *-ing* (*king, ring*).

## I Spy a Rhyme

Play this rhyming game with any busy picture. Start by naming an object from
the picture. Invite a volunteer to find and name a rhyming object. Continue,
letting children name objects and rhyming partners. Here's an assortment from
pages 30–31 of *I Spy Fun House: bee/the number 3* and *golf tee, cat/bat, mice/dice,
car/star, stool/tool* (pliers), *chair/bear, cork/stork.*

## I Spy an Inch

Challenge children's observation skills by playing
I Spy an Inch.

 Cut out a one-inch window from a sticky note
(or index card).

 Invite a child to place the window anywhere
on the page. How many details can he or
she list about what's inside that square? Can
anyone keep going with the same square when
the first child is finished?

 Use the same procedure to continue exploring
the picture. Watch as children's observations
become increasingly detailed.

## Similarities Chain

Ask a child to close his or her eyes and put a finger anywhere on an I Spy
picture. Have the child open his or her eyes and identify the object being
pointed to. Let this child select another child to name something else in the
picture that is like this object in some way. Continue, having children take

# Tip

Children will delight in
taking over the task of
using sticky notes to
suggest mystery objects
for their classmates to
find. No doubt they'll
find even more obscure
objects than you do!

turns identifying objects that have something in common with the last object. Record each object as it is named. At the end, invite children to help each other recall how each object is like the next one.

### Name That Picture!

Notice the names given to each picture in an I Spy book. Talk about how the names fit the pictures. Then let children suggest new names for the pictures in a book. They might team up for this activity, then share their new names with the class and tell how they came up with them. Discuss techniques they used for thinking of names—for example, did they look for rhyming words, words that started with the same beginning sounds (alliteration), or words that describe the objects in the pictures?

### An Alphabet of Objects

Play an alphabet game that encourages children to take a closer look at the ways in which Walter Wick put objects together to create each I Spy picture. In addition to building spelling skills as children record words for objects in alphabetical order, this game is a good way to strengthen observation skills.

- Write the letters of the alphabet on chart paper, leaving space for a word (or more) after each letter.
- Gather children in a circle. Open an I Spy book to a busy picture. Name an object that starts with the letter A and write the word on the chart paper.
- Pass the book to the child next to you. Have that child identify an object in the picture that starts with the letter B and write the word on the chart paper.
- Continue, having children identify objects for each letter of the alphabet and record them on the chart. If children come to letters that they have trouble with, skip them and go on. When you get to the end of the alphabet, go back to those letters and challenge children to take a second look, using their most creative thinking skills to come up with objects for those difficult letters.

### Alike and Different

Strengthen sorting and classifying skills with this activity.

- Display an I Spy picture. Ask: "How are the objects on this page alike? How are they different?"
- After discussing ways the objects are alike and different, decide on some groups to sort them into. Write names for the groups on the chalkboard,

## Tip

Enrich students' I Spy explorations with award-winning software programs based on the books. Titles include *I Spy School Days*, *I Spy Spooky Mansion*, *I Spy Treasure Hunt*, *I Spy Junior*, and *I Spy Junior: Puppet Playhouse*. Like the books, these best-selling programs offer children layers of detail-rich discovery, challenging their problem-solving skills as they solve riddles and more. For more information on specific titles, see pages 33, 40, and 44.

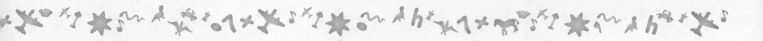

and let children take turns looking at the picture and recording objects that go in each group. Notice the creative thinking at work as children explain their reasoning.

| Red | Yellow | Blue |
|---|---|---|
| numbers on clock | button | marble |
| | letter A | block |
| apple | bead | le |

◉ Are there any objects that don't seem to belong to a group? Invite children to tell why they think they were included.

## Connections Game

Play this game to stretch creative thinking skills.

◉ Start by naming an object in a picture—for example, using the picture on pages 26–27 of *I Spy Mystery*, you might name the yellow sunglasses.

◉ Have the next player name another object that has something in common with this object—for example, the yellow and red ball. (They have the color yellow in common.)

◉ Continue taking turns naming objects that have something in common with the last object named. Be creative—there are lots of ways one object can be like another. Play until you can't add on any more objects, then start over with a new object. It's a different game each time you play!

## What Doesn't Belong?

Gather children in a circle. Open an I Spy book to any picture, and name something that you think doesn't belong and tell why. Pass the book to the child to your left or right and let him or her give it a try. How many objects can children find that they think don't belong? How many different reasons do they have? There are no incorrect answers—just encourage children to explain their thinking. Notice the many creative ways children approach this activity.

## Memory Game

Open an I Spy book to any detailed picture and let children study it for 30 seconds or so. (This works best in a small group rather than with the whole class.) Close the book and ask children to record as many details as they can remember. Now invite children to share tricks for remembering things. For example, children might try to mentally group pictures by color or type. Repeat the activity with a new picture. Was it easier the second time?

# I Spy: A Book of Picture Riddles

(Scholastic, 1992)

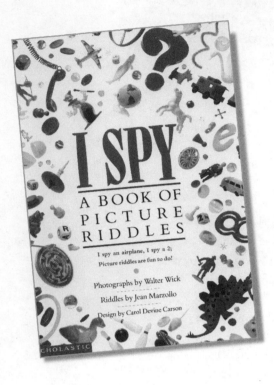

**F**rom a colorful block structure to a sandy beach scene, this book is full of invitations to explore a wide variety of objects arranged in fanciful and fun ways. The pictures in this book are some of the busiest, giving children endless opportunities to find many more hidden objects than the ones mentioned in the riddles—and to write new riddles to go with them!

## Sharing the Book

**S**hare the riddle on the cover of the book. Let children find the airplane and the number 2 as mentioned. Then write a collaborative riddle using the objects pictured—for example, "I spy a little shoe and the letter *R*; a yellow mouse and a race car." Before opening the book, invite children who are familiar with I Spy books to share what they like best about them.

## WordPLAY

I Spy books are all about wordplay. Share the riddles in the book, asking children to notice the rhyming word pairs at the end of the lines on each page—for example, on page 10, the rhyming word pair is *cats* and *hats*. On page 11, it's *rolls* and *holes*. Guide children to notice that sometimes the words have the same spelling pattern, as with the *-at* word family in *cats* and *hats*, but not always. Let children look at the pictures to find other rhyming word pairs—for example, on pages 16–17, they can find *word* and *bird* as well as *glitter* and *critter*. Which words have the same spelling pattern? Which don't?

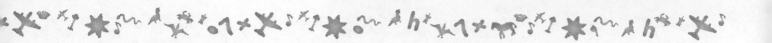

## More I Spy

Invite children to make new discoveries in I Spy pictures. Have them record their findings on chart paper, along with the page number on which they made the discovery. (See examples, right.) Children will enjoy checking the list for new challenges they can try.

| I spy a car, a boat, and a train car that are in more than one picture. | (pages 8–9 and 30–31) |
| I spy the word *handy*. | (pages 12–13) |
| I spy a seahorse reflection. | (pages 14–15) |
| I spy a tiny butterfly. | (pages 26–27) |

Extension Activities

## Nature Word Wall ( ✎ LANGUAGE ARTS, 🪐 SCIENCE)

Children are drawn to nature. They look with endless wonder at butterflies and other tiny creatures, marvel at how big leaves can grow, and never tire of collecting pinecones and other treasures from the ground. Use the picture on pages 22–23 as inspiration for a picture word wall that builds science vocabulary. Remind children to use the word wall as a spelling reference when they are writing about nature, for example, in their science journals.

◎ Start by asking children to name objects they see in the picture, such as pinecones, leaves, flowers, a butterfly, feathers, seeds, moss, ferns, a bird's nest, an egg, rocks, and sticks. Record their words on half-sheets of drawing paper.

◎ Let children each choose a word to illustrate. (Have them do this directly on the word card.) Display your illustrated word wall around a window or in another available space at children's eye level.

### Block-Building ( SCIENCE,  MATH)

Invite students to take a close look at the picture on pages 8–9. Direct their attention to one part of the block structure, and ask them to tell how they think Walter Wick got the blocks to balance. For example, in one tower he balances rectangular blocks horizontally on top of a vertical base. Why don't the blocks topple over? (*Each block is centered on the one beneath, distributing the weight evenly on both sides. This demonstrates the concept of center of gravity—the point on an object where the weight is spread evenly.*) To help children understand the concept of gravity, try this demonstration:

- Ask children to stand and lift their left foot up and out to the side. Invite them to describe how they keep their balance.
- Now ask children to move to a wall. Have them turn sideways and position their right foot and right shoulder against the wall and keep them there as they again lift their left foot up and out to the side. What happens? (*It is impossible to do because they can't adjust their bodies to maintain balance, or center of gravity.*)

### Classroom Cubbies ( LANGUAGE ARTS)

Does the picture on pages 24–25 remind your students of anything in their classroom? Perhaps they have individual cubbies shaped like the cubbies in this picture. Or maybe there are cubbies for art supplies. Invite children to write riddles about the objects in their classroom cubbies. For more fun with cubbies, give each child a copy of page 16. Let children fill in the cubbies with small pictures cut from magazines, then write an I Spy riddle to go with them.

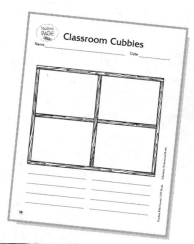

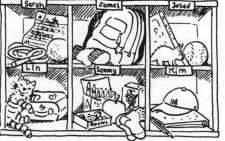

I spy Sammy's snack,
a spare pair of socks,
a new box of crayons,
a collection of rocks.

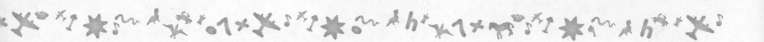

## Snake and Spell ( ART, ✎ LANGUAGE ARTS)

Children will enjoy practicing spelling words when they can use clay snakes to form letters.

◎ Ask children to find the letters made from clay on pages 16–17. What word do they spell? (*sky*)

◎ Give each child a handful of clay. Show children how they can roll the clay into long, thin pieces. Invite them to use their clay "snakes" to make letters. Can they spell their names? How about their spelling words?

## Make a Fan ( ART)

Share the picture on pages 16–17. Ask children to find two fans and to tell how they think they were made. One has tiny sections cut from the paper for a lacy effect. Let children make their own lacy fans by following these directions:

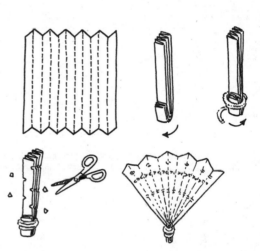

◎ Fold a sheet of paper accordion style (about an inch for each fold).

◎ Fold one end of the folded paper up. Wrap a pipe cleaner around this end.

◎ Snip small sections from each edge of the paper, above the pipe cleaner, being careful not to cut through the paper.

◎ Pull apart the folds to complete the fan.

## Order in the Classroom ( ✳ SCIENCE, 🖩 MATH)

Strengthen sorting, classifying, and organizing skills with an I Spy game that will get the room cleaned up!

◎ Take a look at the picture "Odds and Ends." Ask children to pretend that all of the objects were jumbled in a junk drawer. Now have them pretend that they are the junk drawer organizers. How would they sort the objects into a drawer organizer (the kind with separate compartments for keys, paper clips, rubber bands, and so on)?

◎ Identify a corner of the classroom that needs organizing—for example, the art center, a pile of materials that have accumulated on a shelf, or a supply cupboard. (Or just go for the entire room!)

◎ Say "I spy..." and name something that needs to be put away in the right spot. Let a volunteer find the object and place it where it belongs. Have this child provide the next I Spy clue, and call on a volunteer to find the object and put it away. Continue until the designated area is organized!

# Tip

Children can write a poem or letter on their paper before folding it into the fan (without snipping the edges). They can wrap their fans in paper they decorate and tie the ends with ribbon to make lovely gifts.

# Classroom Cubbies

Name _____     Date _____

_____     _____

_____     _____

_____     _____

_____     _____

# I Spy Fun House

(SCHOLASTIC, 1993)

**Y**ou can almost see yourself in the fun-house mirror, hear the circus band, and smell the popcorn and peanuts in this sensory-rich book. From one page to the next, readers are treated to the sights, sounds, and smells of an amusement park fun house, complete with a mirror maze, magic show, creepy crawly cave, and more. It's a colorful collection, with plenty of playful pictures to inspire I Spy adventures.

## Sharing the Book

What's a fun house? Let students share what they know before introducing this book. Read through the table of contents in the book to paint a more complete picture of a "fun house." To set the stage for this book, fill your classroom with the familiar amusement park aroma of freshly popped corn— and then enjoy it with students while you try some of the activities that follow.

## Word PLAY

I Spy rhymes often employ alliteration—words that are close together and repeat a beginning sound. Invite children to listen for words like this as you read aloud the riddles in *I Spy Fun House*. "I spy a banjo, a bird...," "A button, a B...," and "A man with a mop, and the man in the moon" are just a few of the examples they might find. Let children signal when they hear words that have the same beginning sound—for example, by waving both hands above their heads.

## More I Spy

Invite children to make new discoveries in I Spy pictures. Have them record their findings on chart paper, along with the page number on which they made the discovery. (See examples, right.) Children will enjoy checking the list for new challenges they can try.

| | |
|---|---|
| I spy a camouflaged ladybug. | (pages 10–11) |
| I spy the words FUN HOUSE in mirror-writing. | (pages 12–13) |
| I spy a game of tic-tac-toe. | (pages 20–21) |
| I spy three kinds of balls. | (pages 30–31; golf ball, baseball, gumball) |
| | |

## Tip

Children can play this memory game on their own, using a busy picture in any of the I Spy books.

Extension Activities

## Creepy Crawly Memory Game ( SCIENCE)

Sharpen observation skills with a memory game that uses the picture on pages 26–27. Let children study the picture for 15 seconds. Then have them close their eyes while you cover up one of the creepy crawlies with a sticky note (trimmed to size). Have children open their eyes. Who can guess which creepy crawly is under the sticky note? Let children take over, taking turns covering up a creepy crawly while their classmates guess which one it is.

## Word Builders ( LANGUAGE ARTS)

How many letters of the alphabet can students find in the picture on pages 10–11 (inside the clown's mouth)? Provide children with newspapers and magazines and invite them to cut out letters in different shapes and sizes. Let them arrange and glue the letters on paper to spell words, starting with their names. Have them incorporate the letters and words in an illustration like the one in the book.

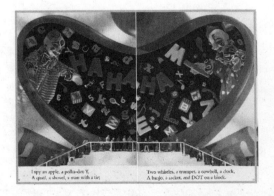

I spy an apple, a polka-dot Y,
A quail, a shovel, a man with a tie;

Two whistles, a trumpet, a cowbell, a clock,
A banjo, a rocket, and DOT on a block.

## Stuffed Animal Sort ( ✍ SCIENCE, 🖩 MATH)

Invite children to bring in a stuffed animal for an activity that strengthens observation, sorting, and classifying skills.

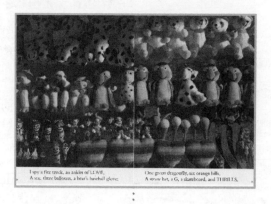

I spy a fire truck, an anklet of LOVE,
A six, three balloons, a bear's baseball glove;
One green dragonfly, six orange hills,
A straw hat, a G, a skateboard, and THRILLS.

- Share the picture on pages 28–29 (Prizes to Win). Ask children what they notice about the arrangement of the prizes. (*They are grouped by type—for example, by Dalmatians, bears, monkeys.*) Encourage children to notice any exceptions to these rules. (*For example, there's a Dalmatian in between a group of parrots.*)
- Invite children to bring in a stuffed animal from home. Have extras on hand to make sure that each child will have one.
- Use yarn to make several large circles on the floor. Ask a volunteer to describe the features of his or her stuffed animal and place it in a circle. Have children who think their stuffed animals go in this group place them in the circle.
- Invite another child to describe his or her animal and place it in a new circle. Again, have children who think their animals belong in this group place them in the circle.
- Continue until every child has placed his or her animal in a group, or until you have children remaining who don't think their animals belong in any of the existing groups. Challenge children to find a way to group any remaining animals, and then review the characteristics of each group.

# Tip

Before children dismantle the groupings to take their stuffed animals home, they might like to experiment with new groupings, based on different attributes they identify.

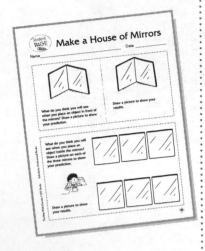

## Make a House of Mirrors ( 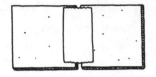 SCIENCE)

Invite students to try to follow what's happening inside the mirror maze pictured on pages 16–17. Then explore the science of reflection by making simple mirror houses in the classroom.

◎ Give each pair or small group of students three small mirrors. (See Tip, left.) Give each child a copy of page 21.

◎ Ask students to place two of their mirrors facedown side by side, leaving about 1/8 inch between them. Have students tape the backs together, as shown.

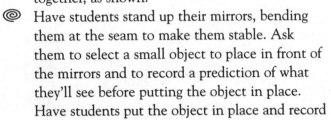

◎ Have students stand up their mirrors, bending them at the seam to make them stable. Ask them to select a small object to place in front of the mirrors and to record a prediction of what they'll see before putting the object in place. Have students put the object in place and record what they see. Discuss differences between predictions and results.

◎ Have students place the mirrors flat on the table again and tape the third mirror to one side, again leaving a little bit of space between the mirror edges. Show students how to stand up the mirrors, bend them at the seam to make a triangle, then tape the remaining side closed.

◎ Ask students to record a picture prediction of what they'll see this time. Then have them place the same small object inside their mirror houses and record what they see. Does it look like there are more images of the object this time? Invite students to try counting the number of images they see, then experiment with placing other small objects inside their house of mirrors.

◎ Discuss the science behind what students see. (*Mirrors reflect images of the objects to make it look like there is more than one of each.*) Ask: "What do you think you would see if your mirror house had four sides?" Test it out!

◎ For more fun, invite children to create a patterned floor covering for the inside of the mirror houses. For example, they might place their mirror houses on paper they've colored with red and yellow stripes (like the mirror maze in the book). How does this change what they see?

# Tip

Try these science supply sources for inexpensive mirrors:

Delta Education
(800) 258-1302
www.delta-education.com

Edmund Scientific
(609) 547-8880
www.scientificsonline.com

The Magnet Source
(800) 293-9190
www.shopinbox.com

# Make a House of Mirrors

Name _____    Date _____

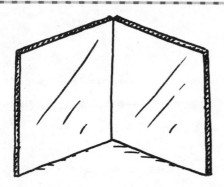

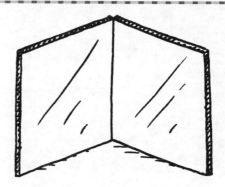

What do you think you will see when you place an object in front of the mirrors? Draw a picture to show your prediction.

Draw a picture to show your results.

What do you think you will see when you place an object inside the mirrors? Draw a picture on each of the three mirrors to show your prediction.

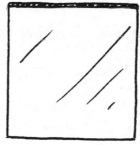

Draw a picture to show your results.

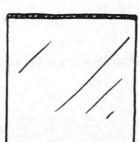
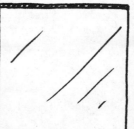

# I Spy Mystery

(Scholastic, 1993)

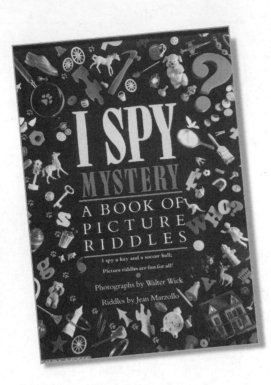

**Y**oung children enjoy a mystery—whether it's decoding a secret message, playing 20 questions to guess the person, place, or thing someone's thinking of, or simply locating a missing shoe. Like putting the last piece of a puzzle in place, solving a mystery provides great satisfaction—and motivation to solve another. This book is full of mysteries for children to solve. They'll peek through keyholes to solve a birthday mystery, investigate shadows to find a monster, poke around an attic in search of a ghost, examine dozens of marbles for clues to a missing ring, and more!

## Sharing the Book

Let children use their own words to explain the word *mystery*. Ask children to be detectives and take a close look at the cover for objects that relate to this theme—for example, the magnifying glass, the key, the boarded-up house, the question mark, the word *Who*, and the puzzle piece. Provide "detective" props children can use when exploring this book—for example, a magnifying glass and notepad for recording clues.

## WordPLAY

Challenge children to be "word detectives" with this book. Start with this assignment: Find all of the words in the riddles that have double letters. (*hammer, rabbit, button, greeting, letters, squiggly, carriage, missing, dollhouse, spoon, wedding, proof, roller, soccer, ball, three, puzzle, egg, fishhook, butterfly, fiddle, kittens, mittens, bell, bubble, bee, moon, broom, glitters, rooster, little*) For an extra challenge, can students find a word with double letters that appears three times? (*the word three, on pages 20, 25, and 28*)

## More I Spy

Invite children to make new discoveries in I Spy pictures. Have them record their findings on chart paper, along with the page number on which they made the discovery. (See examples, right.) Children will enjoy checking the list for new challenges they can try.

| | |
|---|---|
| I spy the same hotdog in two different pictures. | (pages 30–31 and 32–33) |
| I spy a pair of fives and a pair of eights. | (pages 8–9) |
| I spy a domino doorstep. | (pages 24–25) |
| I spy a black cat and six other tiny animals. | (pages 28–29) |

Extension Activities

## Mini Math Mysteries ( ✎ LANGUAGE ARTS, ▦ MATH)

A secret note, a missing key, hidden messages... the pages of *I Spy Mystery* are filled with puzzles to solve. Use one of the pictures to create a math mystery for children to solve. The sample (right) goes with pages 16–17.

Let children use the pictures to write their own mini math mysteries for the class to solve. Have them write the page numbers for the picture they use at the top of their paper. They can write the answer on the back for easy self-checking.

I spy a thimble, a straw hat, a saw,
Six musical frogs, a red lobster claw;

A spoon, a cage, a wedding cake man,
And proof that a cat knocked over the can.

I spy six frogs, two alligators, and a duck. Each has two eyes. How many eyes all together?

## Alphabet Block Spellers ( ✎ LANGUAGE ARTS)

What's the hidden message in the picture on pages 8–9? ("*Find five jacks.*") Give each child a copy of the alphabet blocks on page 26. Have children cut apart the squares and then arrange them to spell the hidden message. Now have them rearrange the blocks to spell new words. How many can they make? Have them record their words and compare them. How many different words can the class spell?

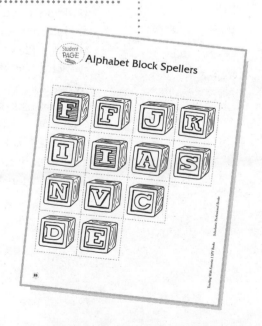

## Use the Clues  (✎ LANGUAGE ARTS)

**U**se the pictures in *I Spy Mystery* for a mystery-writing activity that strengthens attention to detail.

◉ Model the activity by secretly choosing an object in one of the pictures and describing it in a paragraph without naming it. Include such details as size, color, shape, and texture. Let students look at the picture and try to solve the mystery of identifying the object.

◉ Have students write their own mini mysteries based on objects they select from the book. As a clue, they can write the page numbers of the corresponding picture at the top of the page. Have students write the name of the object on the back of their papers for self-checking.

◉ Place students' completed descriptions in a box. Each day, invite a student to randomly choose a mystery from the box and share it with the class. Who can identify the object from the description?

## House of Cards  (✐ SCIENCE, 🎨 ART)

**P**ick up a few decks of playing cards (or invite children to bring in extra decks from home to share) for a construction activity that teaches the science concepts of balance and center of gravity.

◉ Revisit the picture on pages 32–33, asking students to notice the card structures in particular. (There are three.) Invite students to describe how they might go about building a similar structure. Discuss possible approaches to getting the cards to stand up.

◉ Give each child (or team of two) a dozen or so cards. Challenge children to build a structure with them. Encourage them to share ideas as they work. What works? What doesn't? Look for examples of "balanced" cards in students' work—for example, two cards leaning against each other (as in the picture).

### Tip

As they build, encourage children to notice that by building a stronger base, like the structures in the picture, they can be more successful in having their card houses stay up.

## Send a Secret Message ( ✎ LANGUAGE ARTS)

Children will enjoy holding up the picture on pages 26–27 to discover what the secret message on the pink notepaper says. They'll have even more fun writing their own secret messages in mirror-writing. Invite students to write the answer to a math problem, a sentence for a spelling test, or some other assignment in mirror-writing for you to "solve." Respond with a short note—in mirror-writing, of course! For another mirror-writing mystery, prepare a short homework assignment in mirror-writing. Children will look forward to taking out their homework that night to solve the mystery.

## Shadow Mysteries ( 🪐 SCIENCE, 🖩 MATH)

Take a look at the shadowy picture on pages 12–13. Ask students to notice the shadows and tell what they have in common. (*The shadows all face the same direction.*) Review what makes a shadow. (*A shadow is created when an object blocks a light source.*) Make a shadow for students to see. Ask: "In which direction is the light shining to make the shadow you see?" Have students use their observations to guess in which direction the light was shining to make the shadows in the picture. (*from behind each object*) Then let children experiment with objects in the classroom to solve these shadow mysteries:

◎ How can you make a shadow taller? Wider? Shorter? (*by changing the distance and position of the light*)

◎ Can you make a small object have a bigger shadow than a larger object?

◎ Do all objects make shadows that are equally dark? (*No, the darkness depends on the degree of opacity or translucency of an object.*) Are there some objects that don't make shadows? Why? (*Objects that are transparent let light pass through and will not make a shadow.*)

## Book Links

Use *I Spy Mystery* as a springboard for a mystery-reading marathon in your classroom. Along with *Harriet the Spy* and *Encyclopedia Brown*, introduce the offbeat (and scaly) detective in the *Chet Gecko* series by Bruce Hale (Harcourt).

## Tip

Students can use removable wall adhesive or bits of clay to stand up objects and hold them in place.

# Alphabet Block Spellers

Teaching With Favorite I SPY Books    Scholastic Professional Books

# I Spy Fantasy

(SCHOLASTIC, 1994)

**W**hen do toys, kitchen utensils, and cotton balls become cities, space stations, and castles in the sky? Explore these and other imaginary worlds in the pages of *I Spy Fantasy*. There is a city built of blocks, a futuristic space station constructed of kitchen gadgets, a world of unicorns and castles afloat in a cloud-filled sky, an elaborate sand castle, and more. Each scene will inspire children's imagination, letting them make connections to their own pretend play.

## Sharing the Book

**P**retend play is one of the hallmarks of childhood. There are imaginary friends, pies made from mud, and more. *I Spy Fantasy* invites children into other kinds of pretend play with imaginative worlds made from ordinary objects. Take time before sharing the book to let children tell some of their favorite ways to play. Listen for ways that they turn ordinary objects into imaginative worlds of their own.

## Word PLAY

Read aloud the rhyme on pages 16–17 and write it on the chalkboard. Direct students' attention to the words *cart* and *start*. Together, go through the alphabet to find other words that rhyme with these words—for example, *art*, *Bart*, and *dart*. Write them on the chalkboard and guide students to notice the letters that the words have in common (*-art*). Now challenge children to find another word they could use in the riddle in place of the word *start*—for example, *a pan for a tart or a tiny heart*. (The words they choose need to be represented in the picture.) Try the same activity with other riddles in the book.

## More I Spy

**I**nvite children to make new discoveries in I Spy pictures. Have them record their findings on chart paper, along with the page number on which they made the discovery. (See examples, right.) Children will enjoy checking the list for new challenges they can try.

| | |
|---|---|
| I spy a mouse in more than one picture. | (pages 8-9, 14-15, and 26-27) |
| I spy a sandy heart and star. | (pages 20-21) |
| I spy a camouflaged paper clip. | (pages 24-25) |
| I spy a shadowy winged horse. | (pages 30-31) |

---

### Extension Activities

### Block City (👒 DRAMATIC PLAY, ✎ LANGUAGE ARTS)

**U**se the picture on pages 8–9 as inspiration for an I Spy dramatic play center. Invite students to work together to use blocks, toy cars, and other materials in the center to create a busy city. Students can add on each time they visit the center. Set up an easel with chart paper next to the center for posting an I Spy riddle to go with the block city. Change the riddle frequently to encourage students to continue exploring the structure. As an extension, display a word wall in the area to build related vocabulary. Let students suggest words based on the city they've built—for example, *building, street, skyscraper, car, truck, taxi, bus, bridge, tunnel, highway, overpass,* and *underpass.*

I spy two cars, a house and a tree; five squares, a flag, and the letter B.

### Shape Scenes (🖩 MATH)

**A**sk students to look at and identify the shapes that make up the people and animals in the picture on pages 14 and 15. Have them find some of the

---

### Book Links

*Block City,* by Robert Louis Stevenson (Dutton, 1988), is a picture-book version of the classic poem about a young child who transforms his toys into a kingdom. Named a *Parenting* magazine Reading Magic Outstanding Book, this brightly illustrated story is sure to inspire your students' block structures.

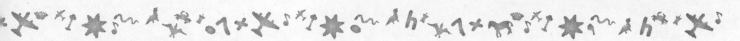

same shapes around the classroom. Then give each child a copy of page 30. Invite children to color and cut out the shapes and then put them together to create pictures. Have students write an I Spy riddle to go with their pictures. Display the picture riddles on a bulletin board, or bind them to make a class book.

## What Sticks? What Doesn't? (✍ SCIENCE)

The scene on pages 16–17 includes lots of objects made from metal. Which ones do students think a magnet would stick to? Bring in an assortment of kitchen utensils, including, for example, lids from canning jars, colanders, graters, ice cream scoops, spatulas, whisks, and funnels. Give each child a copy of page 31. Ask children to record a prediction for each item: Will it stick to a magnet? (yes or no) Have them test out their ideas and record results. Let children go further by using what they've learned to select a few additional objects that they think a magnet will stick to. Have them record the name of the objects and their predictions and results on the back of the record sheet.

## Compound Puzzles (✍ LANGUAGE ARTS)

From *birdhouse* to *gumball*, this book has compound words in many of its riddles.

- Introduce compound words with the riddle on page 8. (You might copy it on the chalkboard.) Invite children to find the word that is made by putting two words together. (*birdhouse*)
- Ask: "What other words can I make with the word *bird*?" That's not so easy, but children might think of *birdcage*, *birdbath*, *birdseed*, even *birdbrain*! Now try making more words from *house*—for example, *firehouse*, *playhouse*, and *schoolhouse*.
- Once students understand the concept of compound words, let them work in teams to find as many compound words in the book as they can. (It's helpful to have multiple copies of the book for this.) Let students share the words they find (*mailbox, horseshoe, pinecones, flashlight, shoelace, gumball*). Then brainstorm more words they can make from parts of each compound word.
- Make puzzles by writing each part of the compound words on index cards. Place the word cards at a center and let children visit independently or in pairs to put the puzzles together.

# Shape Scenes

# What Sticks? What Doesn't?

Name _____     Date _____

| Objects | Predictions Will the magnet stick? | Results Did the magnet stick? |
|---------|------------------------------------|-------------------------------|
|  |  |  |
|  |  |  |
|  |  |  |
|  |  |  |
|  |  |  |

# I Spy
# School Days

(Scholastic, 1995)

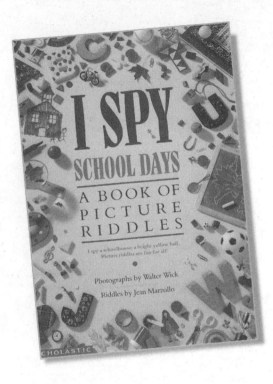

**A**lphabet letters, patterns, puppet shows, playground fun...picture riddles of these and other familiar school-time activities celebrate learning and invite discovery. Each picture has many layers of learning built in—for example, the balloon popper picture lets children make predictions about what will happen as a ball rolls down a chute. In doing so, they'll discover much about the world of levers and pulleys—and the satisfaction of problem-solving to make ideas work.

## Sharing the Book

What kinds of objects do students think they'll see in the pages of *I Spy School Days*? Invite them to look around their classroom and list objects that they might include in such a book. Encourage children to watch for these things in the book as they explore each picture. What's familiar? What's not?

## WordPLAY

Use the picture on pages 10–11 to inspire word games like this one: Read the words on the snake. (*slide, glide, hide*) Can children think of other words that rhyme with these? (such as *tide, wide, ride, side, pride, bride*) Draw a snake shape on the chalkboard. Write the word *snake* inside. One at a time, let children add an *-ake* word to the snake. Make more word family snakes. Try a different phonogram each time.

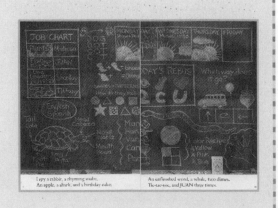

## More I Spy

**I**nvite children to make new discoveries in I Spy pictures. Have them record their findings on chart paper, along with the page number on which they made the discovery. (See examples, right.) Children will enjoy checking the list for new challenges they can try.

| | |
|---|---|
| I spy a camouflaged bee. | (pages 14–15) |
| I spy "Science Is Fun." | (pages 16–17) |
| I spy two words that rhyme with *spy*. _____ and _____ . | (pages 18–19) |
| I spy the word *stegosaurus* eight times. | (pages 24–25) |

Extension Activities

## Teaching With the Poster: Sorting and Classifying
(▦ MATH, ✎ LANGUAGE ARTS)

The I Spy poster, bound in the center of the book, features a favorite picture that is packed with teaching opportunities. Display the poster, and challenge children to solve the riddle. Then try these activities to connect language arts, math, and more:

I spy a spider, an ice skate, a rake, Two bracelets that match, a trumpet, a cake; A dime, the Big Dipper, three flowerpots, A coat with four buttons, and ten paper dots.

SCHOLASTIC

- ◎ Writing I Spy riddles means finding sets of objects with names that rhyme. Sometimes that means being creative! Name an object in the picture—for example, a bright yellow shoe. Challenge children to find a creative way to name something in the picture that rhymes—for example, "letters to spell *boo*." (There's a B among the objects for 5, also two Os in the box for 12.) Let children continue, taking turns naming an object and one that rhymes. For a greater challenge, have children try to match the number of syllables in the rhymes.

- ◎ Invite children to describe the picture on the poster. (It's got boxes for each number 1–12, with objects in each that represent the corresponding number.) Set up another 12 boxes. (Clean pizza box bottoms work well.) Let children work with partners to create a display for the next 12 numbers (13–24). Arrange the boxes and let each team write an I Spy riddle to go with the new set of numbers.

## Tip

Sharpen skills in spelling, reading, writing, math, visual discrimination, and more with the software program *I Spy School Days*. This award-winning program invites children to explore 10 brain-building play areas, including Oops Hoops!, which challenges them to look for objects with shared characteristics, then place them in the appropriate hoops. Successfully solving riddles lets children earn treasures for creating their own I Spy picture riddles.

## Alphabet Art (✎ LANGUAGE ARTS, 🎨 ART)

**A** is for Alphabet, B is for Balloons, C is for Cold, D is for Dots. On pages 8–9, students will see each letter of the alphabet decorated with a corresponding picture. Let them name the picture for each letter, and then create their own ABC pictures. Give each child a block letter traced on tagboard. Have children fill in the letter with pictures of something that represents it. Cut out the letters, and let children take turns placing their letters in order on the chalkboard tray, completing the sentence frame "[letter] is for [object]" as they go. Use the letters to play word games—for example:

◎ For a fun way to line up that also teaches alphabetizing skills, shuffle the letters and give one to each child. Have children arrange themselves in alphabetical order as they line up. For a change, have them go from Z to A.

◎ Place the letters at a center. Let children arrange them to spell big, bright words. Have them record their words on chart paper. What's the longest word they can spell without repeating letters?

◎ Place the letters in a bag. Randomly select a letter. Use that letter to play "I'm Going on a Trip." Start by saying "I'm going on a trip and on my trip I'm going to bring [something that starts with the target letter]." Have a volunteer repeat the sentence, including your word, and then add another. Continue until everyone has had a turn. If children run out of words to name, select a fresh letter and start with the next child.

## Getting the Job Done (✎ LANGUAGE ARTS, 🔬 SCIENCE)

**S** hare the picture on pages 16–17 with children. Explain that this kind of contraption is called a Rube Goldberg. It accomplishes something (popping the balloon) in a complicated way that could have been done more simply. Let students trace the Rube Goldberg path and explain what happens at each step. Then invite them to design their own Rube Goldberg inventions—creating a contraption that accomplishes an ordinarily simple task (such as feeding the dog or sharpening a

pencil) in a roundabout way. Have students diagram their inventions and write a detailed description of what happens from beginning to end. Display diagrams and descriptions along with the picture in the book.

# Tip

## Mail for Me? (✎ LANGUAGE ARTS, ✿ ART)

Everyone likes to get mail, and the picture on pages 20–21 will inspire lots of letter writing, especially when students have their own mailboxes and card-making supplies. For each mailbox, cut a "door" in one end of a covered shoe box. Staple a tab of sturdy cardboard just above the door. (Children will use this to open and close their mailboxes.) Have children decorate their boxes, if desired, and write their name above the door. Stack the shoe boxes to make post office boxes. Stock a nearby table with paper, envelopes, doilies, ribbon, scissors, crayons, and other art supplies. Invite children to make and send each other cards and notes.

To make sure everyone's getting mail, have children draw names out of a hat. In addition to other cards they might like to make and send, they can make a card for the child whose name they selected.

## In or Out? (🌐 SCIENCE, 🖩 MATH)

Invite children to revisit the picture on pages 30–31. Can they figure out how the objects in each circle are grouped? How are the objects in the sections where circles overlap alike? For example, point out the yellow circle in the center. Ask: "How are the seven objects in this circle alike?" (*They have something to do with a circus.*) Now look at the objects in the intersecting green circle. Ask: "How are they alike?" (*They are all people.*) Finally, point out the area where the yellow and green circles overlap. Ask: "How are the two objects in this section alike?" (*They are both people, so they fit in both the yellow and green circles.*)

For independent exploration, give each child a copy of pages 36 and 37. Have children color and cut out the objects on page 37 and sort them into the circles on page 36, placing objects that fit in two groups in the overlapping section of the corresponding circles.

In or Out?

# In or Out?

Name _____     Date _____

# In or Out?

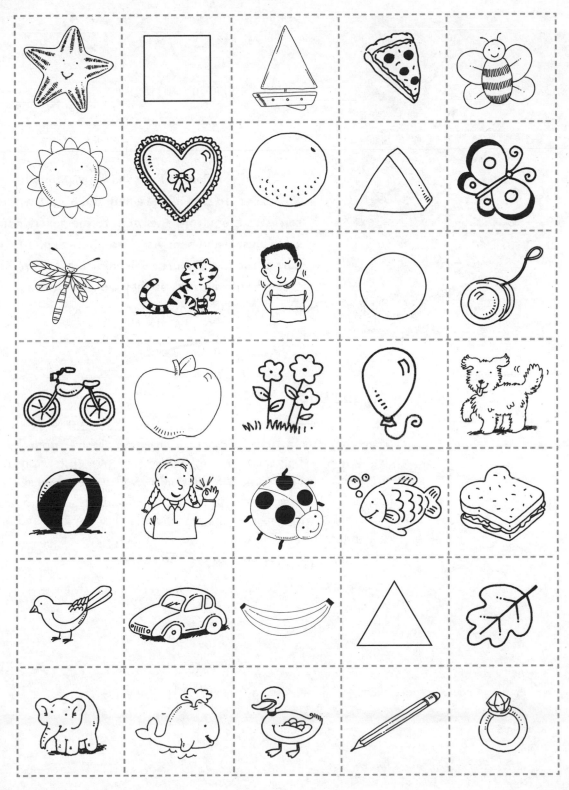

# I Spy Spooky Night

(SCHOLASTIC, 1996)

**E**nter if you dare..." *I Spy Spooky Night* invites readers to step inside a haunted house, where a skeleton leads them from one room to the next. Finding that same elusive and bendy skeleton in each picture is just part of the fun! Children will enjoy making predictions throughout this book as they wonder what spooky scene awaits them with the turn of each page.

## Sharing the Book

**S**et the scene for this book by setting up a "spooky night" corner in the classroom. Drape a dark-colored sheet or length of fabric from the ceiling (well below lights). Pull apart pieces of cotton (purchase it in a roll) to make plenty of cobwebs in the corners. Stuff a pillowcase or sheet to make a ghost. Sprinkle some fake bones about (stuff the ends of paper towel tubes with newspaper, then cover with paper and paint), and add plastic spiders and other spooky night creatures. Before you begin, let students guess what they'll find inside the house that is pictured on the cover.

## Word PLAY

Ask students if anyone knows what a palindrome is. If anyone in the class has a name that is a palindrome (such as *Bob* or *Hannah*), use it as a clue. After everyone knows the meaning (a word that is spelled the same forward and backward), share the pictures and riddles on pages 12–13 and 22–23. Can students find the palindromes on these pages? (*mom* and *lion oil*) Give students copies of page 41. Have them fill in the blanks to complete the palindromes in the picture. (*Madam, step on no pets, Hannah, 37973*) What other palindromes can students find in the picture? (*wow, Otto*) When they're finished, have them glue the picture to a larger sheet of paper and write a riddle to go with it.

## More I Spy

Invite children to make new discoveries in I Spy pictures. Have them record their findings on chart paper, along with the page number on which they made the discovery. (See examples, right.) Children will enjoy checking the list for new challenges they can try.

| I spy two numbers that add up to 36. | (pages 18–19) |
| I spy 8 two times. | (pages 28–29) |
| I spy BOO and a sock for a shoe. | (pages 30–31) |

---

## Extension Activities

### ABC Cleanup ( ✎ LANGUAGE ARTS)

Do your students' rooms ever look like the one on pages 30–31? Clean up with an alphabet game! Start by saying "It's time to clean my room. I'm going to pick up…" Then name something in the picture that starts with A—for example, *an animal.* Let a volunteer continue, repeating the sentence and your word, then adding one for B—for example, *a black cat.* Keep going, letting children add on as many objects as they can. If they're stumped, encourage creativity. For example, H could be *howling ghost,* Y could be *yellow birdie.*

### Spooky Night Recipes ( 🖩 MATH, ✎ LANGUAGE ARTS)

Use the Ghost Recipe on page 22 of *I Spy Spooky Night* as a springboard for making a spooky snack (not to be eaten, of course). Ask children what kinds of potions they imagine could be cooked up with the contraptions in the picture. Read the Ghost Recipe together and ask what part of the recipe might be missing. (*the directions*) Share some real recipes as models, then invite children to create their own recipe for a spooky snack. Remind them to tell how much of each ingredient and to include directions. Have students illustrate their recipes; then bind them to make a Spooky Snack Recipe Book.

## Book Links

For more fun with palindromes, share the following books by Jon Agee:

*Go Hang a Salami! I'm a Lasagna Hog! and Other Palindromes* (Farrar, Straus & Giroux, 1992)

*Sit on a Potato Pan, Otis! More Palindromes* (Farrar, Straus & Giroux, 1999)

*So Many Dynamos! And Other Palindromes* (Farrar, Straus & Giroux, 1997)

### Creaky Gate Symmetry ( ▦ MATH, 🎨 ART)

What do students notice about the creaky gate on pages 8–9? Record all observations. Then take a closer look at the symmetry, starting with the stone structure on either side and the baseball atop each, then moving on to look at the number of posts on each side of the gate and the designs between them. Notice places where the gate design is not symmetrical—for example, in the cat, owl, seahorse, and other objects that are hiding here and there. Let students learn more about symmetry with the gate pattern on page 42. Ask them to design their own symmetrical Creaky Gate scene. Have students glue their pictures to a larger sheet of construction paper and add a riddle to share with classmates.

### Creepy Crawly Adjectives
( ✎ LANGUAGE ARTS)

I Spy Spooky Night is full of creepy crawly adjectives. Use them to introduce this part of speech—and to have some fun using words that describe.

- Use the riddle on pages 8–9 to introduce adjectives. Explain that adjectives are words that describe nouns. Invite children to find the adjectives on this page. (*Broken* describes *bone*, *busted* describes *seam*, and *silent* describes *scream*.)

- Let students go on a word hunt to find other adjectives in the riddles on each page. List the adjectives on chart paper, along with the words they describe—for example, *hidden door* (page 17), *skeleton key* (page 21), and *ghostly sail* (page 24).

- Now let students create their own riddles for the pictures, using as many adjectives as they can—for example, to go with pages 12–13: "I spy a shadowy cat, a creepy spider, and a quiet mouse; a dusty stairway, a watchful owl, and a tiny tree house."

- For a challenge, invite children to describe a single noun with more than one adjective. (See page 22 for an example: "short sad poem.")

## Tip

Pair *I Spy Spooky Night* with the award-winning software program *I Spy Spooky Mansion* for more intriguing adventures. Children will need to make their way through 10 creepy rooms—solving riddles and secret messages to find their way out. Along the way, they'll strengthen skills in reading, vocabulary, writing, following directions, logical thinking, and more.

# Playing With Palindromes

Name _____

Date _____

Teaching With Favorite I SPY Books Scholastic Professional Books

# Creaky Gate Symmetry

Name _____

Date _____

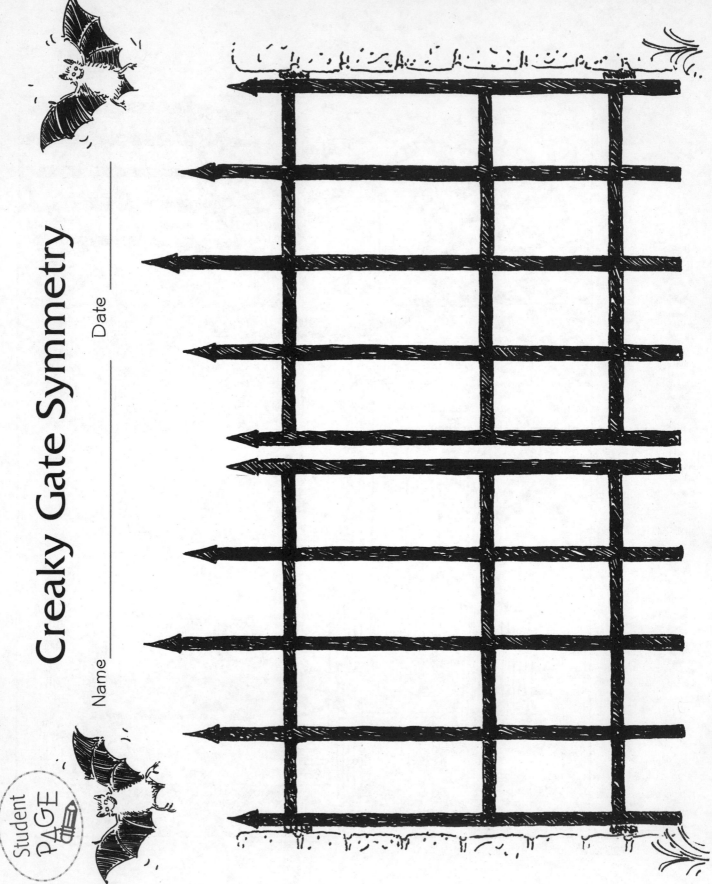

*Teaching With Favorite I SPY Books*    Scholastic Professional Books

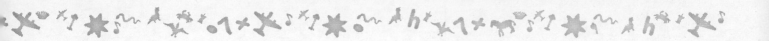

# I Spy
# Treasure Hunt

(SCHOLASTIC, 1999)

Treasure hunts evoke a sense of adventure—there are maps to read, clues to follow, and, of course, the prospect of gold (or other goodies if you're not a pirate). All of these things naturally appeal to children, who are rewarded not only by the treasure at the end of the hunt but by the satisfaction they feel from reaching a goal. *I Spy Treasure Hunt* has all this and more, in pictures and riddles that take students to a small seaside town where they'll go from one place to another as they search for a hidden treasure.

## Sharing the Book

Introduce *I Spy Treasure Hunt* with a treasure hunt that leads to a copy of this inviting book. Write clues on slips of paper that take children from one spot to the next and eventually to the book—for example, "There's a clue in a place where you could wash your face." To make sure each child gets a chance to help solve a piece of the puzzle, have groups of two to three children take turns following each clue.

## WordPLAY

*I Spy Treasure Hunt* is set in a village called Smuggler's Cove. Let students browse the book, looking for names of places, including Fish House, C. Worthy & Sons, Anchor Marine, and Duck Pond Inn. As you record the names for places on chart paper, ask students if they notice anything about them. (*The first letter in each word is capitalized.*) Let children group the places they've named—for example, by places people eat, places people shop, and places people stay. Let children think of names for similar kinds of places where they live. Have them record these names on chart paper, being careful to use capital letters.

## More I Spy

Invite children to make new discoveries in I Spy pictures. Have them record their findings on chart paper, along with the page number on which they made the discovery. (See examples, right.) Children will enjoy checking the list for new challenges they can try.

| | |
|---|---|
| I spy Lighthouse Point on all of these pages: | 14–15, 16–17, 20–21, 22–23, 26–27. |
| I spy a paper clip fence. | (pages 20–21) |
| I spy ten things that start with the letter B on pages 10–11. | bicycle, books, boat, boy, bird, bench, blue overalls, bumper, branch, ball) |

### Extension Activities

## Treasure on the Playground! ( SOCIAL STUDIES)

Use the map of Smuggler's Cove to introduce a mapmaking activity that invites students to imagine there's buried treasure on their playground.

- Ask students to take a close look at the map of Smuggler's Cove (pages 14–15). Have them name details that make the map helpful for finding one's way around—for example, roads, buildings, bridges, and the coastline.
- Take a walk on the playground or other school area. Ask students what kinds of details they would include on a map of the area—for example, a swingset, trees, signs, and a slide. Ask: "If you were a pirate burying your treasure on this playground, where would you put it?"
- Let students consider the question, then give them each a copy of page 47. Have children map the playground area and then write a riddle that gives clues to the "hidden treasure."
- Display students' maps, and let them solve each other's riddles to find all the treasures!

## Tip

Children will eagerly continue their explorations of pirate history with *I Spy Treasure Hunt*, a software program based on the book. Winner of numerous awards, including the 2001 Parent's Choice Software Award, this program challenges children to solve riddles to uncover pieces of a treasure map. Along the way, they'll investigate an island, a lighthouse, a museum, the coastline, and more than a dozen other spots in Smuggler's Cove. There are three different treasure-hunting paths to take in this absorbing adventure, each with a new set of clues to solve.

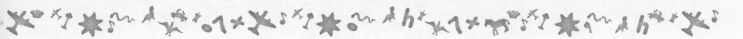

## Symbols at Sea (ART, SOCIAL STUDIES)

**C**an students find a pirate's flag in the pages of *I Spy Treasure Hunt? (There's a Jolly Roger on pages 12–13 and on 14–15.)* Let students guess what pirates' flags symbolized. (*They warned ships at sea to surrender.*) Ask students to tell what other flags—for example, their country's flag— symbolize. Let children create flags or banners with symbols that say something about themselves or their class. Use the flags to create a class or hallway display.

**Tip**

These flags make a colorful display at open-school night. Children will enjoy challenging their families to guess which flag is theirs.

## Tracking Down Treasures (MATH, LANGUAGE ARTS)

**P**lay this twist on a familiar game to practice giving and following directions as well as using coordinates on a grid. For a more challenging version, add on to the grid— for example, making it 15 x 15 or 20 x 20.

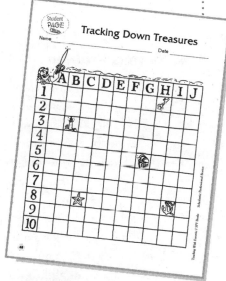

- Give each child two copies of the reproducible grid on page 48 and a file folder. Have children tape the grids to the inside of a file folder, as shown.
- Make a few extra copies of the grid and cut them into "treasure chests" that are each three squares wide and two squares high (for a total of 6 grid squares). Give each child a treasure chest.
- Have children partner up to play, sitting back to back so that they can't see each other's game boards. To begin, each child hides the treasure chest on the grid, placing it evenly over any 6 squares and taping it in place. Players then take turns naming coordinates on their partner's grid in order to locate the hidden treasure. Students can record correct and incorrect guesses on their other grid, using a different color for each. The winner is the first player to locate the 10 points that outline the treasure chest.

**Tip**

To make reusable game boards, laminate the grids on the file folders. Students can use wipe-off markers to mark their treasure chest locations. For more fun, suggest that students hide more than one treasure chest, each a different size.

Where in the world were pirates? The Caribbean, Mediterranean, and Aegean Seas, the Baltic Sea, the Indian Ocean, and the China Sea to name just a few places. Learn more with *Eyewitness Books: Pirates*, by Richard Platt (Dorling Kindersley, 1994). For a more light-hearted look at pirates, try these titles:

*Do Pirates Take Baths?* by Kathy Tucker (Whitman, 1997)

*Everything I Know About Pirates: A Collection of Made-Up Facts, Educated Guesses, and Silly Pictures About Bad Guys of the High Seas* by Tom Lichtenheld (Simon & Schuster, 2000)

## Shipwreck! ( SCIENCE,  LANGUAGE ARTS)

Have students find a picture of a pirate's ship in *I Spy Treasure Hunt*. (There are several in the map on pages 14–15.) Investigate words for parts of a ship, including *port* (left side), *starboard* (right side), *stern* (back), and *bow* (front). Reinforce ship vocabulary—and listening skills—with this lively game:

- In a large, open space, use string to outline a "ship." Have children identify the port, starboard, stern, and bow, then gather on one part of the ship and "hit the deck" (sit).
- To play, call out the name for one of the three areas in which children are not sitting. Children need to then jump up and go to that area. The last one to sit is out.
- The game continues in this way until only one child is left. To keep everyone in the game, let children who are out take turns calling out the next move. To keep everyone on their toes, call out "Hit the deck!" once in a while. When they hear this, children need to immediately sit wherever they are, and again, the last one to do so is out.

## A Pirate's Problem (  MATH)

Gold coins, gems, pendants, pearls...Invite students to take a look at the treasure on pages 30–31 and guess what a treasure like this might be worth. Let students share their ideas, then try this activity to put themselves in the place of pirates dividing their treasure.

- Set the scene for pirate math problem-solving by filling a small chest (or bucket or box) with "treasures." Craft-store gems, coins, marbles, beads, and chains will all add to the effect. Place a value on the treasure—say, one million dollars (or any other number you want children to work with).
- Pose a pirate's problem: "If everyone on the ship's crew [students in the class] receives an equal share of the treasure, how much will each person get?"
- Have students calculate their answers (possibly working in pairs), and then share their results and method.
- Try a reverse problem: "If there are [number of students in the class] in the ship's crew, and each person gets a share worth $ [a number you want students to work with], how much is the entire treasure worth?"
- Let students calculate and share their answers, again explaining their methods. Then let them create their own pirate problems. Students can put a twist on their problems by considering additional information. For example, they might decide that captains get more than crew members.

# Treasure on the Playground!

Name _____     Date _____

# Tracking Down Treasures

Name _____ Date _____

|    | A | B | C | D | E | F | G | H | I | J |
|----|---|---|---|---|---|---|---|---|---|---|
| 1  |   |   |   |   |   |   |   | 🔑 |   |   |
| 2  |   |   |   |   |   |   |   |   |   |   |
| 3  |   | 🏰 |   |   |   |   |   |   |   |   |
| 4  |   |   |   |   |   |   |   |   |   |   |
| 5  |   |   |   |   |   |   | 📦 |   |   |   |
| 6  |   |   |   |   |   |   |   |   |   |   |
| 7  |   |   |   |   |   |   |   |   |   |   |
| 8  |   |   | ⭐ |   |   |   |   |   | ⚓ |   |
| 9  |   |   |   |   |   |   |   |   |   |   |
| 10 |   |   |   |   |   |   |   |   |   |   |

Teaching With Favorite I SPY Books   Scholastic Professional Books

# I Spy Super Challenger!

(SCHOLASTIC, 1997)

Children like a good challenge—especially one that is just the right size (not too easy, not too hard). Whether the challenge is actually met or not, the idea of giving something your best shot is a valuable lesson. Setbacks give children a chance to revise their problem-solving strategies. Successes build confidence and interest in seeking new challenges. *I Spy Super Challenger!* features a collection of some of the most complex pictures from other I Spy books, along with riddles that will challenge every child.

## Sharing the Book

As you get ready to introduce *I Spy Super Challenger!*, let students take a quick look through the pictures. Invite them to tell what they remember about the pictures—for example, children might mention some of the strange places they found the objects mentioned in the original riddles. Sharing these observations builds language skills as children have a chance to express ideas in different ways. As children revisit the pictures and take a closer look, they'll make new observations. This encourages initiative and perseverance and helps children grow as independent learners.

## WordPLAY

Give each child a sheet of paper. Have children trace one of their feet and cut out the shape. Now share the riddle on pages 10 and 11. Ask children what they think "a trotting globe" might look like. (*a wind-up globe with moving feet*) Can they find it in the picture? Let children show what the word means by "trotting" around the room. Now brainstorm other words for the ways people can move—for example, *run, skip, jog, walk, march, race, hop, tiptoe, stomp*. Let each child write one of the words on his or her foot shape. Display the feet around the room, taping them heel to toe to "walk" them around the walls.

## More I Spy

**I**nvite children to make new discoveries in I Spy pictures. Have them record their findings on chart paper, along with the page number on which they made the discovery. (See examples, right.) Children will enjoy checking the list for new challenges they can try.

| | |
|---|---|
| • I spy the numbers 1–9. | (pages 10–11) |
| • I spy a tiny boot and its match. | (pages 8–9) |
| • I spy a camouflaged dog. | (pages 14–15) |

---

**Extension Activities**

---

## Tip

## Storybook Theater ( ART,  LANGUAGE ARTS)

**I**n the picture on pages 18–19, how many characters from favorite fairy tales and fables can your students name? When they exhaust the possibilities, turn a couple of appliance boxes into a classroom storybook theater that will capture students' imagination and attention, while reinforcing reading, writing, listening, and speaking skills.

- Cut out and set aside one side of an appliance box. (Actors will enter through here.) Cut away the top half of the opposite side to make a stage area.
- Cut a second appliance box into two sections (two sides each). Attach to the left and right of the stage area, as shown.
- Cut a decorative "topper" from the remaining cardboard.
- Invite students to paint the theater, adding a name to the topper and pictures of characters and settings to the front and sides.
- Post a sign-up sheet so that students can plan ahead for their performances. You might set aside time on Fridays for these events.

## I Spy Categories ( ✎ LANGUAGE ARTS, ▦ MATH)

The objects in the picture on pages 26–27 are already divided into groups. But are there other ways to group them? A game of Categories teaches categorizing skills, extends vocabulary, and strengthens spelling. It's always fun, too!

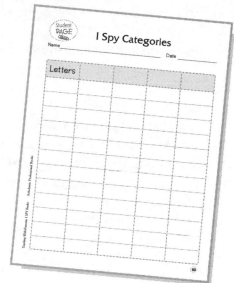

- ◉ On index cards, write headings such as Animals, Colors, Indoor Things, Outdoor Things, Toys, and Things That Move (one heading per card). The more headings you have, the more students will have to choose from. Make a set of alphabet cards, too—one letter per card. Leave out letters that may be too difficult to match to objects, such as Q, W, X, Y, and Z.

- ◉ Give each child a copy of page 53. Select four heading cards and have children write them in the spaces across the top of the chart. Select five letter cards and have children record them in the spaces on the left side of the chart.

- ◉ Display the picture on pages 26–27 (or any other picture). Have children fill in names for objects in the picture that fit each category. For example, for the category "Toys" and the letters D, P, C, B, and T, a child might name domino, peas, car, blocks, and train. (Note that objects might fit into more than one category.)

- ◉ Invite children to share their charts. How many different ways did they find to complete each category?

## Tip

For a whole-class version of the game, make a Categories chart on posterboard. Fill in categories and letters (make sure there are at least as many words to fill in as there are students in the class), and display an I Spy picture with it. Let children take time during the day (or throughout the week) to visit the Categories chart and find something to fill in.

## Math Captions ( ✎ LANGUAGE ARTS, ▦ MATH)

Turn *I Spy Super Challenger!* pictures into another kind of challenge: math problems. Open the book to any picture and display it on the chalkboard easel. Ask children to write a math story problem to go with the picture. Have them write the story problem on one side of their paper and the matching number sentence and explanation on the other. Invite children to display their story problem alongside the book, for classmates to solve.

## Book Links

For a look at how one group of children solves an estimation problem, share *The Jelly Bean Contest*, by Kathy Darling (Garrard, 1972). What do your students think of the various strategies the characters tried?

## Tip

Use students' daily estimates for more math practice. What is the lowest estimate? The highest? The average? How many estimates were lower than the actual number? Higher?

### Estimation Station (▦ MATH)

The busy pictures in this book present all sorts of challenges. For example, direct children's attention to the box of marbles on page 31. How many marbles might be in the box? Invite children to share estimates and strategies. Then give each child a copy of page 54. Invite children to guess how many marbles are in this box and to share their strategies. Teach them a "divide and estimate" strategy for making a reasonable estimate: Divide the marbles into approximately equal sections, then count the marbles in one section and multiply by the number of sections. Set up a daily estimation station to strengthen this skill:

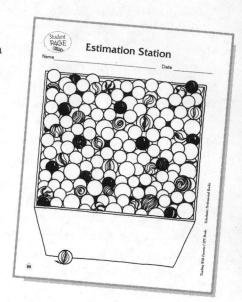

- ◎ Place a box on a table or section of a counter. Label the box "Estimation Station." Place a large, empty envelope next to the box. Label it "Estimation Envelope."
- ◎ Each day, fill the box with a different object—for example, marbles, table-tennis balls, checkers, large beads, maybe even some jelly beans or gumballs.
- ◎ Have children record an estimate of the number of items in the box and place it in the envelope.
- ◎ Check estimates each day, and invite a volunteer to lead the class in using the divide and estimate strategy. Count the items and compare.

# I Spy Categories

Name _____    Date _____

| Letters | | | | |
|---------|---|---|---|---|
| | | | | |
| | | | | |
| | | | | |
| | | | | |
| | | | | |
| | | | | |
| | | | | |
| | | | | |
| | | | | |
| | | | | |

# Estimation Station

Name _____    Date _____

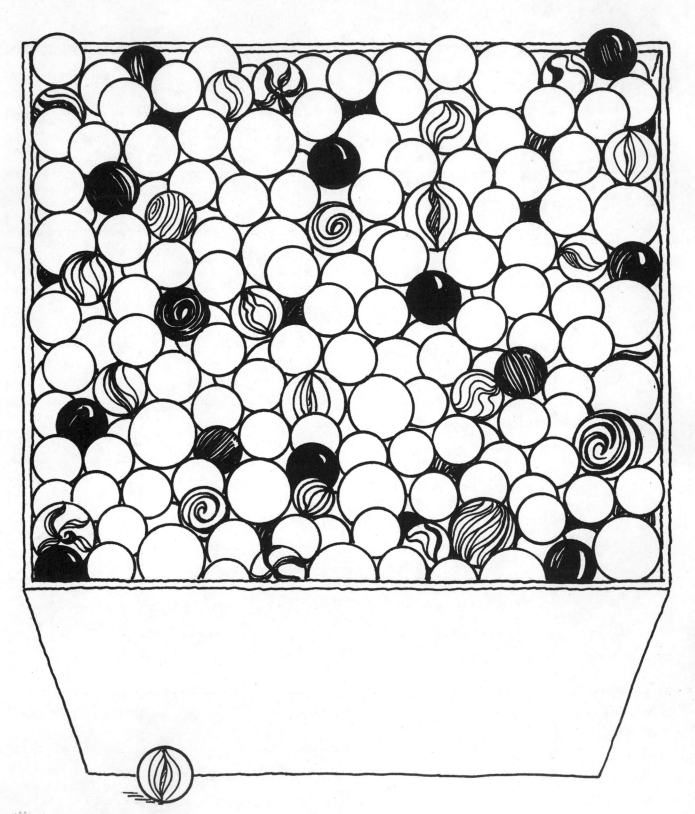

*Teaching With Favorite I SPY Books*    Scholastic Professional Books

# I Spy Gold Challenger!

(SCHOLASTIC, 1998)

*I Spy Gold Challenger!*—the first of the Challenger books—features a new set of riddles to solve for 12 of the most intriguing and complex pictures from other I Spy books. From "56 people" to "toe prints," the riddles in this collection challenge children to find the most elusive of objects, building observation and creative problem-solving skills in the process.

## Sharing the Book

Are your students ready for some superchallenging riddles? Before introducing the book, talk about ways people approach challenges—for example, by teaming up with others or asking questions. Let students share recent experiences of taking on a challenge. What does it feel like when they accomplish a challenge? What can they learn even if they are not successful the first time around? (*for example, to try a different approach and to persevere*)

## WordPLAY

Share the picture and riddle on pages 18 and 19. Is there anything else in the picture that Jean Marzollo could have used in the riddle in place of the word *string*? Start by going through the alphabet to find words that rhyme. Look for matching things in the picture. Encourage children to be creative—they might come up with solutions that have more than one word. Substitute the new word(s) for *string* to rewrite the riddle. Here are two samples (the new part is underlined):

I spy a screw, a skateboard, a spring,
A turkey, a bottle, <u>the first letter of ring</u>.

I spy a screw, a skateboard, a spring,
A turkey, a bottle, <u>a bug that can sting</u>.

## More I Spy

**I**nvite children to make new discoveries in I Spy pictures. Have them record their findings on chart paper, along with the page number on which they made the discovery. (See examples, right.) Children will enjoy checking the list for new challenges they can try.

| | |
|---|---|
| I spy five keys and five monkeys. | (pages 12–13) |
| I spy a word that rhymes with *pool.* | (pages 14–15: *school*) |
| I spy the abbreviations for south and north. | (pages 18–19) |
| I spy three numbers that add up to 14. | (pages 20–21: 9 + 1 + 4) |

## Extension Activities

## Morning Message ABCs ( ✎ LANGUAGE ARTS)

**F**or a morning message that will fire up children's thinking skills for the day, try this:

◎ Open up *I Spy Gold Challenger!* to a busy picture—for example, Cubbies on pages 18–19. Display the picture with your morning message pad. Include in your morning message an invitation for each student to find something for one letter of the alphabet, from A to Z. Write the letters A to Z below your message, leaving room next to each for children to write a word and sign their names.

◎ As students go about their morning routine, have them include a stop at the morning message. Ask them to choose a letter not yet taken, find an object to go with it, write the name for it next to the corresponding letter, and sign their name.

## Shape and Color Connectors (  MATH)

The picture on pages 26–27 is full of shapes and colors, including an intriguing triangle puzzler. Give each child a copy of the triangle patterns on page 59. Guide children to notice that each large triangle has four smaller triangles in it. Ask children to color the triangles, choosing a different color for each of the four smaller triangles. (They should use the same four colors on each set of triangles.) Have children glue the paper to tagboard and cut out the large triangles (leaving the small ones intact). Challenge children to connect the triangles, matching the color of the small triangles on each side.

**Tip**

For an interesting twist, have children use a color and pattern combination for each small triangle.

## Measuring the Balloon Popper ( MATH)

Can students guess how big the balloon popper is (pages 30–31)? Let them suggest estimates; then ask them if there's anything in the picture that might help them make a better estimate. Guide students to notice the ruler. Ask: "How can you use this to figure out the actual size of the entire setup?" (They can mark off the length of the ruler in the picture and use it to see how many "picture rulers" long or high the balloon popper is. They can then convert that to actual feet.)

I spy two pencils, and a porcupine,
Two cups, a nut, and a double nine.

Two straws, wood shavings on the floor,
And something that's also on page 24.

**Tip**

For a related activity, see page 34.

## More Bounce Per Ounce?

( ▦ MATH, 🪐 SCIENCE )

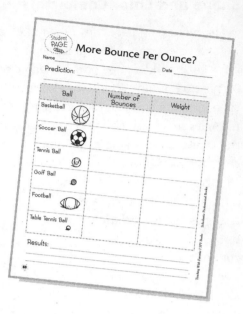

In addition to being a great way to teach compound words (*baseball, football, basketball*), sports are an inviting way to explore math. Have children name the sports they see represented in the picture on pages 8–9. How many of these sports involve a ball? (*baseball, soccer, golf, tennis, pool, whiffle ball, kickball, paddle ball, football, table tennis, and basketball*) Gather as many of the different balls as you can, and surprise students with them one day. After the excitement quiets down, investigate the correlation between weight and a ball's bounce factor.

◎ Begin by asking which of the balls will bounce the most. Ask students to devise a test to find out. (One way is to drop each ball from the same height, say three feet, and count the number of times each ball bounces.)

◎ Before conducting the test, ask students which ball they think will be bounciest. Have them record this on the reproducible sheet (page 60). Let students take turns holding the balls to see which they think is heaviest and lightest. Discuss whether the weight of a ball will affect its bounciness.

◎ Have students conduct the test and record their data. Then weigh each ball in ounces and have students complete the record sheet. Together, compare the number of bounces and weight. You might also use the data to create a class graph.

◎ To go further, have students find out if height makes a difference in the number of times the balls bounce.

## Tip

Introduce the word *sphere* to describe the shape of a ball. Have children work together to write a definition of this geometry term.

# Shape and Color Connectors

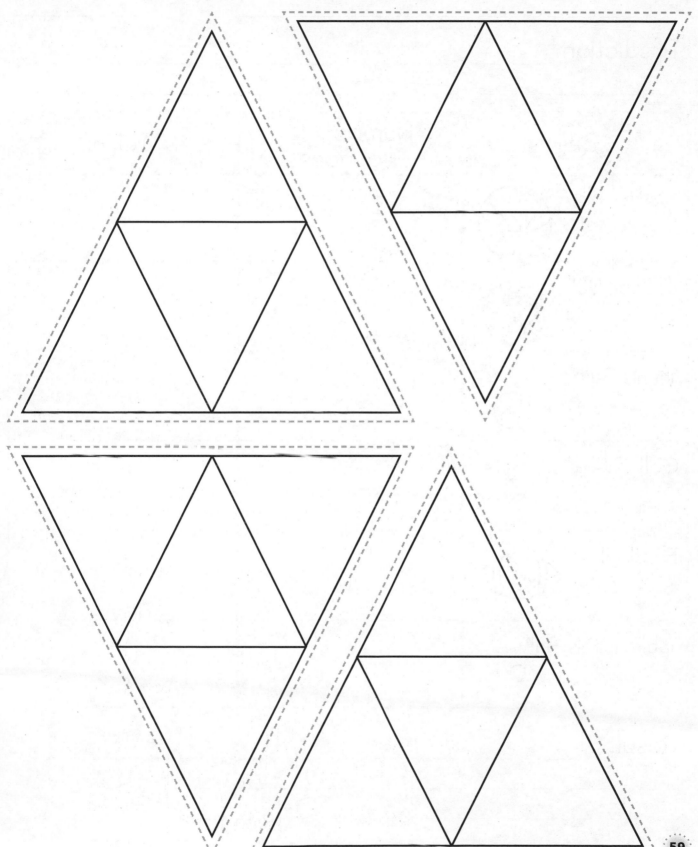

# More Bounce Per Ounce?

Name _____    Date _____

Prediction: _____

_____

| Ball | Number of Bounces | Weight |
|------|-------------------|--------|
| Basketball | | |
| Soccer Ball | | |
| Tennis Ball | | |
| Golf Ball | | |
| Football | | |
| Table Tennis Ball | | |

Results: _____

_____

Teaching With Favorite I SPY Books    Scholastic Professional Books

# I Spy Extreme Challenger!

(SCHOLASTIC, 2000)

The pictures in this book may look familiar, but the challenges are all new. *I Spy Extreme Challenger!* features 12 of the most imaginative, complex, and unusual pictures from previously published I Spy books. The riddles invite children to take a fresh, new look to find even more unusual objects than they did the first time.

## Sharing the Book

Play an I Spy game as a warm-up to *I Spy Extreme Challenger!* Look around the room for something that is extreme in some way—for example, an "extremely big book" or an "extremely long string." Let children take turns naming other "extremes" they see. Encourage them to be creative—for example, they might notice an "extremely wavy line in a picture," an "extremely fast fly on a window," or an "extremely sunny day outside."

## WordPLAY

Children are naturally drawn to extremes—the *softest* stuffed animal, the *tallest* block tower, the *tiniest* bug, the *biggest* leaf, and so on. Use this I Spy book to inspire a list of words that describe extremes—for example, *smallest, hungriest, funniest, happiest*. Record suggestions on chart paper. Explain that words like these compare people, places, ideas, and things, and are called adjectives. Invite children to identify objects in the I Spy pictures, based on some "extreme" quality (the smallest, the biggest, the shiniest, and so on).

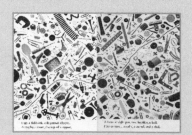

## More I Spy

Invite children to make new discoveries in I Spy pictures. Have them record their findings on chart paper, along with the page number on which they made the discovery. (See examples, right.)

| I spy an extremely tiny hat. | (pages 10–11) |
| I spy an extremely long word. | (pages 14–15) |
| I spy two ways to tell time. | (pages 18–19) |

Children will enjoy checking the list for new challenges they can try.

---

---

### Extension Activities

### Button, Button ( ✎ LANGUAGE ARTS, 🔬 SCIENCE)

There are lots of buttons in the picture on pages 16–17. Use them to play an attribute game. Start by secretly selecting a button. Give students one clue at a time as they try to guess the button. For example you might offer the following clues: *round, not yellow, not red, two holes, smaller than a dime, smooth.* Once someone guesses the button, let that student take a turn. Now let children challenge each other with a bigger assortment of buttons. Give each child a copy of page 64. Have children color in the buttons, being as creative as they like. (You might bring in a jar of buttons for inspiration.) Let them pair up to play the game with their new button collections.

---

### Prickly, Sticky, Scaly ( ✎ LANGUAGE ARTS, 🔬 SCIENCE)

The picture on pages 10 and 11 is full of textures. Play a game to introduce words for the way things feel.

◎ Say a word that describes a texture, such as *prickly*. Invite a volunteer to find something in the picture that might feel this way. (*the strawlike packing material*)

- Have this child say another word for a texture, such as *soft* or *feathery*. Let this child call on a volunteer to find something in the picture that might feel like this. (*feathers*)
- Continue letting children take turns naming textures and asking class-mates to identify corresponding objects in the picture. Addition words include *sharp* or *spiky* (dinosaur's spikes), *rough* (rope), *cool* (aluminum can), *fuzzy* (pipe cleaners), *sticky* (paint), *smooth* (paintbrush handle), and *scaly* (alligator's skin).
- Create a class I Spy display with new objects that represent these and other textures. Write a riddle to go with it, being sure to incorporate descriptive vocabulary for the textures.

## Details, Please  (✎ LANGUAGE ARTS)

Post a daily "extreme" challenge based on the pictures in *I Spy Extreme Challenge!* You might tell children what page the object appears on, or you may prefer to have them scour the book. For practice with using detail in their writing, have children describe exactly where they found the object. They can place their descriptions in a box labeled "I Spy Extreme Challenge!" At the end of the day, check students' slips and reveal the object's location. Be sure to read some of the descriptions aloud to share the ways students are using detail in their writing. Sample extreme challenges follow.

- I spy D O T (pages 12–13)
- I spy SWAN. (pages 14–15)
- I spy an ace. (pages 18–19)
- I spy a hidden heart. (pages 26–27)

## How Old Is She Now?  (▦ MATH)

Have children find the dated photograph on page 30. What do they think the date corresponds to? (*the date the photo was taken*) Have students pair up to solve a related math problem. Ask: "If the girl in the photo was five years old when it was taken, how old would she be now?" Have students work together to solve the problem. To stretch students' thinking and reinforce reasoning skills, invite them to solve the problem a different way. Bring students together to share their thinking, method, and solutions. How many different ways did they find to approach the problem?

**Book Links**

To keep your classroom I Spy challenges going, use the activities in this book as inspiration for teaching with the following titles:

*I Spy Year-Round Challenger!* (Scholastic, 2001)

*I Spy Ultimate Challenger!* (Scholastic, 2003)

# Button, Button

Name_____  Date_____